Unsaid

Some tease, provoke, entice
Some run away, some hide.
A memoir of my thoughts...
The ones that I could catch.

Asmita Rajiv

You can reach the author at:

asmita@asmitarajiv.com
www.asmitarajiv.com
Instagram @asmita.rajiv

ISBN 9798671104028

FIRST EDITION

To Rajiv

However high my dreams may take me, my soul
always returns home to you. You are the strength
behind my quest to take my flight higher and my roots
deeper.

To everyone

Who were an inspiration for my paintings, prose
and poetry. Who lent me their eyes and heart so that
I could see and feel the world in a million different
hues.

Dear fellow travellers,

As Maya Angelou said:

"Life is not measured by the number of breaths we take, but by the moments that take our breath away."

Indeed. So beautifully and simply captured and yet so difficult to pursue. We are so pre-occupied by the monotony of our daily existence, that often the moments that take our breath away are perhaps the ones where we are actually holding our breath owing to some anxiety. Where then, is the time to pause and smell the proverbial roses?

As we live our lives in this rigmarole, the constant jolt of our thoughts and emotions to our senses leaves us even more overwhelmed. So much so that the only easy way out is to shove these thoughts and emotions under the carpet of our minds and to deal with them later, or perhaps never.

But we forget that these thoughts are still inside our minds. We forget that by ignoring them constantly, we are only making them more desperate to be heard and felt.

What if, when the next time these gems come knocking, we open the door and let them in. What if, instead of ignoring them, we acknowledge their presence and gather courage, patience, and compassion, to look them in the eyes as an expression of how we have been living, thinking, and growing as individuals.

Some may dismiss this as a bothersome exercise; but as for me, I write.

'Unsaid' is an account of my conversations with my mind, in no particular order of time. Some of these thoughts were initiated as a result of my personal experiences, while many others emerged from struggles shared by people around me.

No matter the origin, they surely helped me understand myself and others a little bit better. They helped me make sense of the different ethos that makes people react differently to the same situation.

By penning down these thoughts, it is my effort to share with you some of the understanding that I could garner, that helped me make a little more sense of the numerous strings of life pulling us in different directions.

In no way am I trying to impart any kind of wisdom or have any false notion that I know the answers. On the contrary, I know with certainty that I am a long way from having the answers.

I offer this book as a memoir of my own learnings and realizations, with a hope that maybe these thoughts will speak to you in the same way they spoke to me. And however sketchy or incomplete these learnings might be, I offer them with complete humility and gratitude.

If you could take a few moments to hold these thoughts, embrace them, feel them, and reflect upon them, maybe you would find your own unique interpretation coyly hidden in these words. Maybe some of these words will gift you your eureka moment as they did for me.

As I opened my eyes to the world that I knew
The echoes of my voice, as clear as morning dew

The words that I spoke
Since I thought I made sense
From the time I became me
Till right now, in my present

These words that I hear
I would like to share with you
'Cause the echo of my world
May resonate with yours too.

I hope they will. I know they will.

Yours truly,
Asmita

How is this book structured?

It is not.

I would urge you to treat the flow of these thoughts like a river flowing through stretches of the varied landscape. Sometimes gushing down from rocky mountains to serene valleys, from wild forests to calmer plains, from rustic villages to glamorous cities; constantly changing its moves, moods and rhythm.

This book is best read a few pages at a time. I would urge you to pick up any page, open your heart to whatever presents itself, and to give it a chance to speak to you.

Embrace it for as long as you wish, reflect upon it for as long as you desire, before you are ready to move on to the next page.

> *Getting lost in the world of words*
> *I let my heart freely roam*
> *Often then, through a different path*
> *In so losing, I find my home.*

My company
my thoughts
my silences ...

Sometimes
that's all
I need

Closed eyes

Speak to me, he whispered in my ears
Share your words, however few
Does your heart, beat for mine?
Can you hear mine, beating for you?

Speak to me, I whispered in return
What we have, is that enough ?
Will it last when the sun goes down
Will it fade when the rays fall tough?

And as we spoke to soothe the aches
A meagre few words reached the other
Some got lost in the crowd of noises
Others fell prey to the filter between ears

But when the eyelids draped the vision
Surrounding quietness gathered around
Our hearts then covered a million miles
And finally, we heard their beating sound.

Fact or Fiction?

The mind is our personal realm of wizardry, where we not only close our eyes to reality and call it an illusion, but also weave our favourite stories and believe them to be the reality. The more adept we get at this sorcery, the harder it gets for us to distinguish between what is a fact and our interpretation of it. Our inner world becomes a cloak of so many self-conceived truths that it conceals who we truly are, not just from the world, but also from our own selves.

Our vivid stories give birth to a false self that we present to the world as the real us. Every time we cover our eyes with a patch of a new story, we begin to see the illusion of ourselves that we created for others. Slowly, we start losing sight of the real us. So enamoured are we by the beauty of our patches, that we forget, however colourful they may be, they still blind our vision.

Disservice to Self

One of the biggest disservice
we do to ourselves
is to continue
cradling denial.

Pain that sings

From pain and sadness come the most beautiful, soulful, and meaningful words.

That may be because, in the moments of happiness, we are so engulfed in enjoying the emotion at a peripheral level, that we forget to dive into the depth of its roots.

Pain and sadness, on the other hand, do not give us a choice. They pull us right from our core and throw us into their alchemy, till the time every iota of our being is drenched in them.

And then, when the words come out, they create soulful poetry.

The Courage to Love

Having the courage to love,
even when we know
that it'll be short-lived,
is perhaps
one of the greatest wounds
and the greatest healing
we can gift to our heart.

Only You

In the arms of his mother
With back turned to his toys
Clinging to her tightly
He whispers, this little boy

"All my favourite toys together
Do not give me the love that I get from you
O Mother, my dear mother
All I really need is Only You"

Curving and tilting sharply
To give comfort and hear his laughter
She stands unwavering
Enduring the pain of awkward posture

To her baby she says,

"In this journey of my existence
Whatever life brings to you
For the rest of my life, my love
I'll always be there for Only You".

Diving Deep

Often many do not dive deep into a relationship for fear of getting their hopes and hearts broken. But the question is not whether that may or may not happen, because it most likely will.

The question is, whether despite that, is it still a worthwhile journey to pursue? The question is, when we keep a broken heart and a fulfilled heart on the opposite sides, which way will the balance tilt.

To discover the beauty that lies in the ocean's depth, we have to let go of the safety of staying afloat.

Diving deep doesn't always mean sinking, it just means we need to learn to swim better.

Being Unreasonable

Sometimes being unreasonable
is the only reasonable alternative left,
to fight for something that's worth fighting for.

New Paths, New Decisions

Today, we are who we are, and have what we have, because of the sum of choices that we made in the past. Some were forced upon us by our circumstances, some were rooted in the depth of our beliefs, and some rested on the shoulders of our priorities. But regardless of how they were thrown at us, it was we who caught them.

But that was then. And this is now. If today we are not happy with where our decisions have brought us, it is time to make some new choices and choose some new paths. But this time, what if, instead of spreading our arms to catch whatever comes our way, we let the wisdom of our soul and the honesty of our heart decide what to pick. What would it be like, if for a change, we let the heart indulge in its dreams wholeheartedly and choose without fear.

Maybe that's when our choices will feel like home.

What Matters

The only thing that matters is
how heartily we are living
the only life that we have.
The rest is nothing but just filling gaps.

Her Myriad Hues

She has more facets than one
She does more than she can for everyone
She brings hope, joy and life to her dear ones
In return she swallows dark from their cauldron
The colours covering her face, are your cues
They tell the story, of her myriad hues.

The Adventure

When the heart is chosen over the mind to lead the way, it is a journey we seldom forget.

It is a wanderlust of gratification, self-expression, enrichment, and ardour. An escape from the carefully manicured lawns to the laid-back expanse of the wilderness. A transition from a handful of measured steps to an endless unimpeded run. A deviation from plush, velvety landscape to arid, thorny terrain.

Sure enough, we return home wounded, but never empty-handed. We bring back with us a bouquet of scars, each raring to tell an unforgettable story.

The Toughest Battles

The toughest battles are the ones
that are fought in the labyrinth of our minds.

Desires

Why do we tend to stack our desires in the same bin as sin?

When we consider a simple act of relishing a dessert as an indulgence, when we describe a sumptuous cake by the word 'decadent' (meaning corrupt, immoral, self-indulgent), it's no wonder that we associate our more significant desires with even greater guilt or remorse.

What is it about our desires that make them tainted in our own eyes? Is it that our desires are unrighteous for us, or is it that we have not built ourselves righteous and worthy enough for them?

The Gem

If you meet someone with whom you can connect intellectually, emotionally, and spiritually, treasure that person with all your sincerity. In a world full of shiny stones, it is no easy feat to find a real gem for yourself.

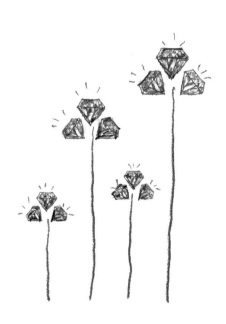

The Autumn Leaf

Once upon a time
There was a me

Wandering about in stupor
Through some lit and unlit gashes
Between shiny and duller patches
Minding my own business
Finding my own bearings
Treading as taught and learnt
On wavy mounds of greenery

And like always
I played my favourite game of hopscotch
The hopscotch of my life

cont.

And as I bent to pick up my pebble
I saw the fallen autumn leaf
There, it lay...

Quivering yet unafraid
Completely devoid of any shame

For the leaf knew, that it's okay
To rest when fallen down
To surrender to the meaning found
To let the earth embrace its pain
'cause in healing there is no shame

When I turned the leaf over
I found my face smiling back at me
And just like that on that autumn day
I found a piece of my broken me.

Settling for Less

When it comes to our career, money, and success, we don't want to settle for anything less than the picture-perfect life. We leave no stone unturned to be ahead of the rest of humanity. But when it comes to our relationships, we often give up too quickly.

We look around our world and gather evidence to a half-hearted life with shallow and unfulfilled connections. We convince ourselves that it is the way of the world. After all, the majority can not be doomed or delusional. So very promptly, we reach the conclusion that this is the best we will ever get.

And we stop trying.

cont.

We stop trying to search for the person who we are truly meant to be with.

Perhaps, that person is hiding inside our current companion, desperately waiting to be seen, heard and re-discovered by us.

Or perhaps that person is somewhere still out there in the world searching for us.

Either way, we will never know unless we stop settling for less.

A Fulfilled Life

How fulfilled we live our lives, depends upon

    - the strength of our dreams, and

    - the constraints of our beliefs

Too Honest

There's no such thing as 'being too honest.' Honesty is just '*plain vanilla*' honesty. It is how honesty is delivered, and how it is received, that changes its flavour from vanilla to '*bitter cocoa*' or '*sweet cookie dough*'.

If the speaker takes care to be honest without being inconsiderate, and if the receiver takes care to listen without weaving stories, then honesty can be given and taken honestly.

Ice cream anyone?

Inside the Mind

To delve deeper inside our minds with complete honesty is an act of bravery. For we may not be prepared to come face-to-face with what may present itself.

The Journey

What is love if not a journey
With small ripples and plenty big waves
Beginning, if not marked with friendship
Can it carve a steady path ahead?

Along this great adventure
Lie delicate threads of discoveries
Of self, the other, and together
That weaves many soulful memories

Like true friends, if sail along
The love will rise and shine
It will prevail when the youth is gone
And will stand the test of time.

Our Beautiful Garment

The biggest irony of our life is that we, the owner of our body and mind, do not really know the person residing inside it. We believe that who we are is so utterly flawed that we will never receive acceptance from the world if we appear in our naked forms. So, to escape rejection, pain, and shame, we begin to dress ourselves in the gown of our dreams. We keep embellishing our garment by stitching satins of myths, sewing sequins of lies, and embroidering silks of pretence.

But there will be a day when instead of giving us a sense of security, these layers will make us feel confined and claustrophobic. We won't be able to stop ourselves from wondering who was the person we buried inside us.

And that will be the day, we will start ripping the layers apart, one stitch at a time.

Inner World

Only when our inner world sings,
can we hear the melodies of the outer world.

The Canvas of Life

As an artist, it is in my spirit to appreciate all the shades that lie in between the two extremes called black and white. While it comes effortlessly in art, it is the life outside the canvas that needs a mastery to recognize situations beyond the rigidity of black and white.

It requires a consistent and deliberate effort to open up our mental palette and dilute the blacks and stain the whites. It requires patience and courage to look at life in its myriad other hues.

In that sense, we all need to be artists.

Courage is Weak

Courage is weak.

It meekly resides inside all of us.

We just need a strong enough reason to look for it

and bring it out in the open.

We the Pinocchios

We start our humble journey
With fears and few dreams
With our rights and our wrongs
Firmly guiding all our dreams

Everyday on this path
We keep piling up our loot
Success, money, and pleasures
And with them some accolades too

Soon this loot gets heavy
But we don't let it go
Instead we shed the layers
Of moral suit we always wore

cont.

And so goes out of window
Beliefs we held so high
We let go of cherished values
Slowly, one at a time

But the one who's still walking
On thorns of moral ground
We look with awkward glances
We lost, what he has found

We know where this has led us
We know the cost of win
We know we are all Pinocchios
Only he had just one sin.

The Safety Net

To get past the fear, one must believe in something
more powerful than the fear itself. For most, it's God.

For me, on that beautiful September morning, as
I was about to dive down from 15,000 feet above
the ground, what gave me a real sense of faith and
comfort was the miracle of engineering. It not only
made the seemingly impossible possible, but also
safe enough for my hesitating mind to bow down to
gravity.

Not to say that science is more magnanimous than the
Almighty. But at that moment, science felt more tangi-
ble, something that I could touch and feel to ward off
my fear.

In the end, it all comes down to placing faith into one
thing to take a leap of faith into another.

My Tomorrow

I don't know what will happen

in all of my tomorrows.

But as of today,

I am just happy that

whatever happened,

happened.

Accepting or Resigning

There's a clear difference between accepting a situation and resigning to it.

Accepting means admitting the fact that something has already occurred, whether we like it or not. It is akin to acknowledging the reality of the 'as-is' rather than hiding behind any denial. Only after accepting, can the process of dealing with the situation begin. One can then consciously choose which door of possibilities to open, the one that prompts to remain in the status quo or the one that is marked with an exit.

On the other hand, resigning to a situation is to helplessly continue being in the status quo without offering oneself a chance to explore any other possibilities.

Accepting is to give power to oneself, while resigning is to give power to the circumstances.

Exploring

Sometimes, exploring without a purpose

is the whole purpose.

Of All the Times

Of all the times when your presence mattered
This was the time it mattered the most
To help me pick up my fallen pieces
To help me smooth my broken edges

Of all the times I wanted to hear you
This time I yearned for your words the most
To sing to my ears in a soothing sound
To whisper to my spirit that you are around

Of all the times that I needed your strength
This was the time I needed it the most
To help me heal my wailing heart
To help the little angel lovingly depart

Of all the times that I eagerly wanted you
This was the time I wanted you the most
My fingers searching for yours to clutch
Maybe never again will I want you so much.

Having Someone

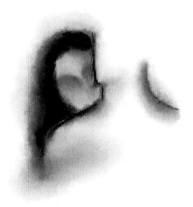

We all have to fight our own battles, carry our own burdens, and confront our own realities. But having someone next to us makes this struggle a little easier.

Steps in the Journey

The journey called love requires the travel companions to take their steps in harmony. How we walk together determines whether this journey feels like a walk in the park or a boot camp.

If a foot is left hanging up in the air for too long, we will stumble and fall. If the foot is kept back at the same place it was lifted from, we will continue marching without moving an inch.

It is therefore essential to pause every now and then to check whether we are walking towards the same destination, and more importantly, whether we are still walking together.

My Pain

If my pain doesn't move you,
we are not meant to be.

Safe Exit

Parting ways hurts. How deep the hurt is depends on how deep the involvement was.

Sometimes to protect oneself from this fall, one gets involved only at a level that offers a safe exit. While this safeguards the heart from a deeper hurt, it also deprives it of a possibility to feel a deeper connection.

It's not an easy choice as both ways it's the heart that is at the losing end.

Tug of War

My mind is where I force myself to live
My heart is where I hope to forever reside
They are distant neighbours sharing a wall
They are often two coins of the same side.

One pulls me towards balancing the weights
Other pushes me into a steadfast disparity
One asks me to carefully tread the greys
The other cherishes colourful unfamiliarity.

These all-consuming forces twist and twirl
Creating tangles of dos and donts
My shoulds and shouldn'ts, fall out of line
In this war of yes-es, and these battles of no's.

The Agony

Despite the agony,

the heart always wants to seek out the adventures of life.

It prefers suffering the pain to wondering 'what if'.

Some Dreams Must Become Reality

We all may not find the courage to live life on our own terms all the time. Often, we are faced with circumstances that prevent us from living the life of our dreams. Some of these hurdles may appear to be so enormous, that we believe them to be invincible. We believe that the cards we are dealt with are the only ones we are ever going to get.

But every once in a while, a few feeble thoughts of a more fulfilled life brave their way through these iron-clad restricting beliefs. These are the times when we must orchestrate a mutiny to transfer the reign of power from our beliefs to our dreams. These are the times when instead of casually dismissing their existence as baseless fantasies, we must salute their bravado, hold their hands and guide them to their dreams.

Some dreams must become reality, no matter what. Especially this one.

The Delay

When we know what our heart truly desires,
by delaying to walk towards it, we are only depriving
ourselves of the fulfilled life that we truly deserve.

Sometimes this is worse than not knowing what the
heart wants.

The Tenants of our Mind

The demons that reside in our minds exist only because we have given them permission to live there. We know that they are parasites feeding on our happiness, yet we extend them a long-term lease to stay. There must be a hefty rent that we are getting from them. An exchange so lucrative that we become their addicts.

Make no mistake, however ugly these demons are, however ferociously they are sucking energy from us, we are no angels either. We too are feeding on them. What could be so important that we tolerate the pain of their existence in our lives? Is it the sweetness of self-pity? The righteousness of a victim mentality? The might of holding power over others?

May be the day we understand what it is that we devour from them, will be the day we can finally ask them to leave.

Claiming Worth

When I see myself, I see a small moon
But Alas,
My moon is not
From the pages of a romantic's world
I see my moon with holes and blemishes
I see my moon withered, grey and cold

To turn my greyness into colourful spring
I begin my search for another grey soul
Never feeling complete just on my own
I need another's void, to make me whole

To pull up my worth, even higher
I have to be taller, than the tallest tree
And so I hunt for a vine to latch on
Or a ladder of souls, a little greyer than me

I know now my need for the crowd
Some for reassuring, I am okay in this birth
Others I need for my ego to build upon
Oh, all this drama, just for claiming my worth.

Being Perfect

I am not trying to be good at being perfect. I gave that up a long time back. But what I am trying to be good at, is to let my uniqueness shine through.

Now, that's an art worth perfecting.

Just a small idea

When an idea begins to take shape in my mind, all that is required of me is to make space for it. For who am I, to come in the way of something brave enough to show it's incompleteness with complete nonchalance.

Tilting towards the Masses

If my **opinion tilts toward those who do not hold** the blessings of the majority, does that make me inconsiderate towards the significant masses? Don't they already have enough numbers in their favour?

Shouldn't the voices of the unheard be amplified?

Watering the Ego

Stereotyping and diminishing another person's identity is often used as a quick-fix solution for glorifying one's own false ego. Stereotyping a single individual or an entire community may start as a harmless humour, but it soon turns into a bigoted satire that is no longer hidden behind subtleties.

As we continue to depend on another's downfall to boost our false pride, we are, in fact, turning our ego into an insecure predator, whose worth is defined by the defeat of others. It may temporarily uplift our self-esteem and give us a false sense of superiority, but in the long run, it will only make us insecure in our true element.

For our self-esteem to be taller, it needs to stand on its own two feet, rather than leaning on the crutches of someone else's wreckage.

Burns like a sting

I see wavering flames in a tiny dark pit
Flames from a fire so small,
That it can hardly be called a fire
But when its fledgling flames
Touch the skin
Oh, it surely burns like a sting.

How can a minuscule spark
Be so ferociously strong
To burn what it touches
And leave a bold scar
From where does it come
I wonder in vain
Slicing my soul
With a knife of it's flame

I silenced cluttering of my mind
My eyes then saw, removing their blind
It's from within me, that the fire springs
No wonder, that it burns like a sting.

An Infection called Passion

Passion is a force that transports people into a surreal world. A world, where they are so utterly engrossed and consumed in being in their true elements, that for once, it does not matter to them what others think. This state is where our hearts speak freely. This state is where our creativity thrives.

When we find our spark fading, flame extinguishing, and inhibition surfacing, that's our cue that our passion is dwindling. In these moments, it is a worthwhile endeavour to be in the proximity of those who exude it all around them. Just by being close to it, passion can spill into our empty spaces and re-ignite itself.

It has that kind of effect.

Happiness & Melancholy

Happiness and melancholy, both are adept at moving someone to tears.

While happiness requires a remarkable moment to pull the strings, melancholy can do the job just by presenting itself in beautifully wrapped words.

Contentment or Excellence?

'Contentment' and 'striving for excellence' need not be at the opposite ends of the tug of war. Even though they may appear to be contradictory, both these states of aspiration can and should go hand-in-hand.

While a drive for excellence is essential for creating the orchard of our dreams, contentment is of paramount importance to sit and enjoy the fruits of our labour, before we continue planting more trees. One need not be sacrificed for the sake of the other. In fact, one must be compulsorily followed by the other.

What is the point of creating an orchard when we can't relax under its shade, enjoy the ripened fruits, or listen to the birds sing?

Who Moves Faster?

"Please return", I plead to the passing time,
but it keeps moving.
Then, it smiles back and says,
"Perhaps it's you who needs to slow down."

Wrapped in Love

You sang to us from the depth of your soul
Your love for us made us complete and whole
You played with us with the joy of a child
You let our imagination go beyond the wild
What you read to us was more than prince and fairy
You imparted your wisdom gently in every story

With heavy heart
You made us face the world alone
But you are behind us
We feel you, we have always known

You wrapped us snugly
In the folds of your life
With you we are rooted
But can still fly high

With you around
Stars always shine from above
With you dear Mom
We are always Wrapped in Love.

Mother's Pride

As a mother, I have come to realize that what gives me an immense sense of pride is when people tell me how my kids have demonstrated qualities of friendship, warmth, and creativity. I have realized that the happiness I derive from knowing this is much greater than the one derived from hearing about their academic achievements.

Being a typical 'Indian' mother who takes pride in the laurels of academic excellence, this is indeed a great revelation for me.

My kids are the same, it's me who has gained a better perspective.

The Game of Finite & Infinite

Love and happiness are infinite.
The only finite, is our time on this planet.
So our whole struggle is about
Somehow fitting the infinite into the finite.

Doing the Right Thing

How do I get the conviction to tell my kids to do the right thing, when after so many years, for me, doing the right thing often falls in the narrow spectrum between 'challenging' to 'extremely challenging'. And there have been more occasions than I would want to admit, when I succumbed to taking the easy way out.

Perhaps this is one of the biggest fallacies of being a parent.

Feeling Deep

Whenever we feel
something deep
inside our hearts,
it is at that moment
we have truly lived.
Rest of the time
we are just passing life by.

The Unique Me

I own my uniqueness in this world
I have now decided to claim my space
Separate from others standing beside me
Who too are eager to outline their place

This space however tiny, is mine
This space is where my star shines

I own the patches of my darkness
That others see as blemishes and cracks
But these patches give my life its depth
These boulders help in etching my tracks

Unattainable,
Just by the pureness of the soul
These are the patches
That make my journey whole.

Our One and Only

To consider one person as 'the one and only' is to put an immense burden on shoulders unprepared to bear it. They are bound to get crushed under its weight. It's best to neither give that crown to someone, nor accept it from another.

It is we, who must be our own 'one and only'. Because when the rest of them depart, our one and only still remains with us. This is a responsibility not to be delegated at any cost.

Our Regrets

There are two kinds of regrets.

One for something that we have done and
one for something that we haven't.
It may not be a bad idea to avoid the former,
but to do the latter, at any cost.

Rooting for Ourselves

We often mistake our current inability to live a fulfilled life, as the only plausible way to live. We take the easy route and define a fulfilled life as the one that makes the society dance, rather than the one that makes our own world sing. Life, which should give us joy, is reduced to a game of mere social survival, a game so addictive that it robs us of our time to unearth, seek, and author our own manual for living. We neglect to acknowledge that the rags we considered as a burden and threw behind, were the fragments of our happiness without which our attire may never be complete.

We willingly sacrifice ourselves in the hope that one day it will all be worth it. Well, that one day is today. Has it been worth it? Are we living a life that feels fulfilled to our own selves, in our own eyes? If yes, bravo! If no, it's time we start rooting for ourselves because no one else will do it for us.

The Wildflowers

The selfless act of blossoming
together with the neighbouring weeds
to make the entire landscape
vibrant with life, makes the beauty
of wildflowers unparalleled.

From Me to You

In the middle of the noises
When chaos seems to run around
I send snippets from nearby life
Sometimes in words, sometimes in sounds

To tell you,
That you were thought of
When I read those words
And your thoughts filled my mind
When that song was heard

And I send the snippets
To also remind you,
That this can not be it
And this can not be all
That there's more to life
Outside your walls

cont.

Something worth pausing for
Something to feel alive
To reconnect with another you
Hidden in plain sight

So do take a pause
For a moment or two
For these snippets of randomness
From me to you.

Equation of Life

Companionship and comforts are two of the most essential variables in the equation of our modern life.

How one experiences life greatly depends on who one chooses to share it with. With the right partner, one can revel even in the bankruptcy of comforts, whereas with the wrong partner, one can be morose even amidst affluence.

Yet, we focus all our energies on chasing the wrong variable of the equation.

Togetherness

Often, togetherness is about
cherishing with each other
the simplicity of the mundane life.
It really is that simple.

Intention vs. Action

When it comes to the matters of the heart, having the right intention and backing it up with action are both deeply and strongly intertwined with each other. One displayed without the other can be perceived as an act of half-heartedness.

When an action is done merely because of expectations and not because of a genuine intention, it feels like music without soul. On the other hand, if there is a genuine intention, but it is not backed by action, it feels like a night without stars. For companionship to grow stronger and hearts to grow fonder, both intention and action need to reside under the same roof.

Without them together, an emotion is left incomplete and unexpressed.

Who We Love

Our heart will love someone,

not because it has to,

but because it chooses to.

It is stubborn that way.

A Puzzle

You woman, who are you?
Why are you known to all as a puzzle?
Why do they find you so mysterious?
Why are you still such a riddle?

Why are there still
So many pieces missing?
And those that are found
Do they really mark your tracing?

Is it because you hide yourself well
Or has no one ever tried harder
To see the moon behind the stars
To go a little deeper, or a little farther
Is it because of countless roles you play
For everyone in your life
Or is it because you give so much of yourself
That what is left is difficult to analyse

Oh woman, why are you such a puzzle?

Being Understood

I am okay if someone understands me and then
chooses to reject my thoughts.
It's being misunderstood
that I am most uncomfortable with.

Vulnerability

To share one's vulnerability requires tremendous courage. But it also demands trust and empathy from the one it is revealed to.

To let its guard down flagrantly, vulnerability requires a safe haven seeded with courage and watered with trust. In the absence of this secure cocoon, sharing vulnerability can feel like an open wound from an awkward fall that subjects the bearer, to embarrassment, pain, regret, and ridicule, all at the same time.

Why does exposing our vulnerabilities seem so frightening that we guard them with utmost passion? It's not that we are the only proud owners of them. Every individual carries their own share of the mental morass that places us all in the same basket.

cont.

Why is it then, that we treat our vulnerabilities weaker than another's? Why do we treat them as so delicate that a gentle blow of air can make them collapse? And even if that happens, why do we have to follow their suit and crumble next to them?

If our vulnerabilities are indeed so fragile, aren't we then fools to build our entire identity on such a weak foundation?

Showing Up

No matter the colours of my emotions,
I show up every time to witness them.
Oh yes, I have seen my rainbow many times over.

Early and Late

Be with me
Early and Late

Early, so I can tell you my dreams
Late, so I see you last before I see one
Early, to stop me from falling down
Late, to catch me as I take the brunt

Early, to start our journey hand in hand
Late, to be next to me as we untie our shoes
Early, so we wear our wrinkles together
Late, so you can let me go before you.

The Ownership Game

No one really belongs to anyone. They choose to give their company and presence to you. It is their prerogative should they want to offer it, and your privilege, should you wish to accept it.

Love can never be a game of ownership.

The Wrong Silence

Beware,

Silence is not always golden.
If exercised at an ill-timed moment,
it can be perceived as an absence of
sensitivity, love, or courage.

Sometimes, all of the above.

Nourishing our Core

Just like we feed our bodies on a daily basis, so must we nourish our inner core regularly. The one residing inside our body, our inner self, needs to be given conscious love and attention. It is definitely not a 'once in a while' or a 'someday/ one day' kind of task.

We must bring it out in the open, soak it in the warmth of the sunlight, bathe it in the cool water of a flowing stream, dry it up in the fresh breeze, drape it in the vibrant colours of flowers, take it on adventures in the wild, immerse it in the effervescent spirit of city life, help it unwind under the shade of a tree, let it be moved by poetry and music, and let it be soothed by the silence.

We need not wait for any special occasion in our lives to make it happen; it's the simple things that our inner self craves. It simply needs to be shown the world and be shown to the world.

Leave

Don't stay where you are not wanted,

be it home or heart.

The Sound of Silence

In the reverberating echo of noises
I long to hear an absent defiance
A silent beat or a soundless note
I long for the sound of absolute silence

What would it be like, how the mind will cope
As a trapeze artist steadying on a missing balance
Or a fish stuck at the edge of waterless waves
The deafening noises in between my sound of silence

What I yearn for is the emptiness of a vacuum
And with it, peaceful humming of reverence
An orchestra of carefully laid out nothings
My very own symphony of absolute silence.

Our Own Company

To truly cherish one's own company,
one must first learn to
brave one's own thoughts,
talk to one's inner voice,
enjoy one's own silence.

Web of Our Beliefs

We keep our chosen beliefs very close to our hearts. Out of the many available options, these handful were either handed over to us by others, or were chosen by our own intellect, to make the journey of our life smoother.

However, instead of using them as helpful guide-lines, we start treating them as our sacrosanct life-lines. We forget that these beliefs were created, not by the unbiased acumen of a supernatural force, but by the biased intellect of ordinary people like us, that too in an era that was drastically different from our current.

Yet, we keep them constantly in front of our eyes as a screen to view life, and in the process lose sight of living freely. We cling onto them with our dear lives, even when these so called saviours turn out to be our most formidable foes.

cont.

To keep our status quo in order, we convince ourselves with a tone of finality: 'this is how things have
always been done', 'this is righteous', 'this is moral', or
'what will others think of me'. We must be watchful of
the beliefs that make us use these narratives . They
are the ones which close doors to our chance of living
life with freedom.

These are the beliefs that have over-extended their
stay in our minds. It's time we serve them notice and
make room for new ones.

Ending Up Alone

If we are scared of ending up alone,
then we have completely failed ourselves.
We have not built ourselves to be the kind of
person we can be friends with.

Love is Blind -1

They say love is blind...

Then why do we see marks, on each other's soul
Why do we measure the depth, of every tiny hole
Why see regret and ugliness, in every sigh
Why does laughter dress in grief, in front of our eyes
Why don't we embrace the darkness, of each other's past
Why not let hurt and grief, disappear slowly at long last

And they say love is blind...

Why not close our eyes, to burdens of unsought dues
Why not choose for once, real greys over illusive hues
Why not hear the euphony
hidden in wrath and cries
Why not heal the crevices
of shattered dreams and broken ties

Yet they say love is blind.

New Beginnings

When is it time to really go separate ways or to really move on?

For some, the realization comes only when they reach their ultimate level of anger, frustration, and bitterness. For some, the awareness comes much before the situation becomes toxic. The former doesn't make the reason for separation more justified, nor does the latter make it more trivial.

Our battles are our own, our journeys are our own, and therefore our reasons are our own. There is no one scale to mark some reasons as more reasonable than the others.

But whenever it is time, we must move on.

The One

The one who understands your
mind, body, and heart...

That's the one.

The Distance

There are times when someone feels so close to the heart that the mere closeness of thoughts is enough to move the physical distance into a null.

But then, there are times when the thoughts and words bring such a disconnect of hearts, that even close proximity feels like a distance that can never be bridged.

The Unbiased Life

The sounds of silence, melancholy and joy,
all come from the same instrument...life.
And life is unbiased.

We all get our fair share.

We the Puppets

In the stage of humanity
We play our parts and fill our voids
We face some truths, but many we avoid

Sometimes angel, sometimes devil
Wearing guises of our pride
Colourful as they all might be
These veils on our faces often misguide

We tell ourselves, that we're mere puppets
And we keep doing, whatever we may please
Shielding our evil, we love so dearly
We pretend that a force is directing all our deeds

cont.

So we jerk around the lives of others
To make them all, dance to our whims
But then, we suffer a similar pain
Slowly burning down, throughout our limbs

And then it dawns upon us, with clarity
That there's no evil outside, with wings
It is just us, the human puppets
We are the ones, pulling each other's strings.

The Clouds over my Head

Self-limiting beliefs arising out of our past experiences and sub-conscious conditioning cast heavy shadows over our current reality. They not only prevent us from enjoying the present moment, but also come in the way of going after our dreams.

Like fools, instead of letting these dark clouds pass so that we can bask in the warmth of the sun right above, we drag them along everywhere in search of sunshine.

I have had my fair share of these clouds and I continue to do so. But for a while now, I have been making sincere efforts to release my grip over them and to let them naturally float away the way they are supposed to.

cont.

I have realized that the more I stop running away
from them, the more eager they are to move on,
on their own. As if all they want from me is a mere
acknowledgement of their existence, a compassionate
greeting, and a friendly nod.

Behind each one of these clouds, is a ray of sunshine
waiting for me. And every time I wave the clouds
goodbye, the sunshine greets me with a smile.

My Thoughts

My thoughts were so loud

that I was afraid

everyone could hear them.

So I told them to whisper.

But now, even I can't hear them.

The Wrinkles of My Body

They embrace tightly, my tired face
Caressing gently like never-ending vines
Cropping from every nook and corner
To hold me together safe in their twines
My very own wrinkles, my very own lines.

They actually seem to be quite fond of me
But I ignore them like forbidden curse
And when they tell me to smile at life
I am worried, that it will make them worse

Some were etched from my smiles and laughter
Some took birth during labour pain
Some gave me company as I waited for my children
To return home safely, as I worried in vain

These wrinkles and marks that cover my body
Are telling my stories of glory and pain
They deserve to be cherished, like precious trophies
Instead I demean their existence in shame.

Acceptance

The more we accept
each fallen piece,
the less broken we are.

Our Empty Spaces

We entered this world complete. The holes that we carry within us are our own creation. It doesn't matter whether the knife was our own or someone else's. But it was we who gave the permission.

Sure, some of these holes might have been carved when we were defenceless. But today we are not. Today, there is no reason why we should continue to blindly gaze into their nothingness. There is no reason to helplessly watch the past dig the abyss deeper.

If these voids are still alive within us, it's because we are the ones breathing life into their emptiness. It's because we are the ones lending our voice to make these echoes reverberate.

It's we who need to close the emptiness and silence the echoes; No one else can do it for us.

Beauty of Darkness

Darkness is beautiful too.
It's just that we see its beauty
only when the light falls on it.

Introspection

The most essential ingredient of introspection is brutal honesty with oneself. However hurtful, nasty, irritating or painful it may be, I never dismiss or suppress my brutally honest inner voice. I listen to it.

I may not always act upon it, but I always listen to it.

And that's why I can say with complete honesty that no one else knows me better than me, for I don't lie to myself.

My life and I

My life and I,
We have fought and sulked
We have thought and mulled
We rebelled and succumbed
We bore each other's brunt
We have seen each other's worse
We have braved each other's curse
But we have finally grown together
My life and I,
We have finally chosen each other

Locked Potential

Finally, the truth dawned upon me like a bolt of lightning. I discovered that my real source of regret was not that I quit my career long before witnessing the success that I was destined to achieve. But my regret was that there was an immense potential left within me that still remained untapped.

The potential that I kept expanding even after saying adieu to my career. The potential that continued to blossom as I began opening myself up to life's invaluable experiences, that spread far beyond the boundaries of a cubicle.

And just like that, my focus shifted from the narrow confines of a corporate career to finding other befitting avenues for unlocking this untapped potential.

And when I opened myself up to the endless possibilities, I found my art quietly waiting for me in the corner.

My Life Mantra

My new mantra of life
"If not here, where?
If not now, when?"

And I am taking it seriously.

Today, I woke up dreaming!

The Cost of Following Passion

Creative people give their hearts and souls to their craft, right from the time of conception of the idea, until the last push, to bring their art alive. These proverbial nine months are nothing short of a ride fused with feelings of excitement, purpose, fear, anxiety, responsibility, and joy. At the end of this process, when they finally present their creation to the world, they are in the dark of what's in store for them. They don't even know whether their labour of love will be received with applause, disapproval, or even ridicule.

Nevertheless, they keep doing it over and over again. Each time gathering enough courage to expose their vulnerabilities to complete strangers.

I guess that's the price one pays to go after one's passion.

Change the Question

Don't always ask yourself, "why".
Sometimes ask "why not".

Unpretentious beauty

Once upon a time, there was a me
Wandering about in stupor
Inside the walls of my fidgety mind
My form lazing on the lap of my sofa
My eyes raring to escape its confines

And like always
They played their favourite game of hop scotch
The hop scotch of eyes
Hopping from one view to another

After moments of restless wandering
They finally rested their gaze on a flower

There it was...

Unpretentious of its beauty
Unaware of its bewitching hues
Daydreaming in its own world
Oblivious to the glancing views

cont.

For the flower knew,
That all that was required from it
Was to just simply be
A life brimming with wild intensity

And even though
Being true to self was painfully tough
Just being a flower was simply enough

And so with efforts of a child's play
The flower pulled beings of all kinds
Butterflies, birds, bees, dew drops
Even roaming pair of my restless eyes

And when I turned the flower with my glance
I found my eyes smiling back at me
And just like that on that spring morning
I found a piece of my broken me.

The Storytellers

While anger and pain towards the cause of our hurt may be justified, the allegations supporting these causes are usually not.

Allegations are often our interpretation of the facts. We become such excellent storytellers that we not only start to fiercely believe in our own stories but are often successful in conning others into believing in them too. We use all our might to gather an audience who not only sympathize and empathize with our saga but even applaud at our masterpiece.

However much it may feel like a soothing balm on our pain, it comes nowhere close to real healing.

Action & Results

The same action will manifest different results, depending on whether it was performed from a place of
fear and resistance,
or from a place of
mindfulness and acceptance.

First Self, then Others

Replenishing our own reservoir first, before filling other's, according to me, is certainly not an act of selfishness. In fact, it is just the opposite.

We must first be happy within, before we can spread it outside; first be in love with ourselves, to be able to give it away; be our own friend first, before offering our friendship to others.

We need to feel complete just on our own, just by ourselves, to offer companionship to others. Else, we will end up being a needy soul clinging onto others, expecting them to complete us.

And that is a fantasy doomed to shatter, for how can one empty soul complete another.

Where am I Headed

I think about my life in the future, not because I have the audacity to believe that it will turn out exactly how I expect it to be. But, rather because I do not want to go somewhere unintended, or wake up from my slumber wondering how I got there.

You and Me

When the head clears
When the chaos subsides
When the clutter quietens
And your mind untwines

I want you to think of us
You and me

Huddled in our togetherness
Nestling in the warmth of belonging
In our world of words and silence
In our world of love and longing

Even when you are busy and occupied
Are stressed and need to do lots
Find just a tiny little moment for me
And fill that with me in your thoughts

cont.

And do take me along with you
When chaos and stress is rife
Because I want to be alongside you
Even in that part of your life

Think of us,
You and me

When you are tired and exhausted
And yearn for quietness and serenity
Take my silence along to your world
And rest there with me for eternity

And do take me along in your thoughts
For we can not always be together
Give me a tiny corner in your mind
And let me reside in there forever.

The Greedy Heart

The heart is greedy. It wants everything without any limits and boundaries. To what extent it is successful in attaining them depends on the limits and boundaries of our mind.

Misty Eyes

The mist appearing in our eyes tells us something profound about ourselves. These drops of water should not be scoffed at as a sign of weakness or fragility. They should be honoured to remind us that under our varied exteriors, we are all humans, that we are not just living, but we are alive.

Alive enough to feel an emotion so deep that all the other senses have no choice but to be standstill, just so that they can listen to the silent exchange between the heart and the eyes, where neither speak, but both listen.

The Black Hole

We open our eyes, to this life of today
We don't like what we have
It's what's missing, that we dismay

Looking far and beyond
With tired searching eyes
It's the future we believe
From where our dreams arise

The 'now' is dark and gloomy
The 'now' is never gay
The pastures of the present
Are greener, but some other day

And each day as we catch it
We look with harsh resent
The reality of the future
Mirrors yesterday's present

cont.

We begin to grasp reality
And see the time we've lost
Hunting for what we all had
Already tucked away in the past

The future is just a bubble
Reflecting empty soul
The outer rings entice us
The inside is a black hole.

Monotony is Passé

2016 has truly been a year of unlearning, re-learning, and new learnings. It was scary, exciting, satisfying, anxiety-ridden, riveting, and liberating.

May all my subsequent years be like that.

What to Choose

Sometimes the choices we are presented with are between least of the bad options rather than the best of the good options.

It is often easier to make a decision in the first scenario. Maybe because we know what we don't want much better than what we really want.

No one is Ever Gone

We carry within us our ancestors. Not just our parents or grandparents, but every single one who came before them. Each has played a role in forming our physical and mental being, in the same way, that we will be doing for the ones after us.

Our ancestors have a home inside us. They continue living through us. Just like we will continue living through our children and their children.

> No one is going anywhere.
> No one is ever really gone.

Am I Really an Idealist?

Am I being an idealist, or are you being someone who has learned to accept compromising with happiness as a way of life?

Me and My Differences

I own the errors of my life
For they too are pieces of my puzzle
Some bury me underneath their burden
Some come on top to let go and unburden

Some keep me wide awake at night
But I still own them, coz they are mine to fight

This tiny space that I call myself
It needs to be cherished and not rejected
Surrounded by tiny spaces of others
This space of mine needs to be protected
From those, trying to make identical everything
Merging my feathers, in the shadow of their wings

cont.

I need strength to protect my differences
For being so very different and unique
And save my oddities from the guilt
And sew them together into a beautiful quilt

I need strength to honour each patch right
And I need strength to hold each stitch tight

I need strength to realize
That no two quilts are alike
That these dark shades and these craters
Belong to me, and are only mine
And till the time death do us part
My darkness alone, can be my sunshine.

Exploring My Limits

Whenever I have challenged myself to explore the limits of my fears and insecurities, a new me has always emerged out of my very own shadow.

The Game of Evolution

As a species, we have proven our prowess at winning the game of evolution against all other species. We left the mightiest of the mighty behind, based on the sheer strength of the three-pound organ resting between our ears. But also residing within us is another formless entity camouflaged in a complex mesh of thoughts. This entity, our mind, too works tirelessly, but often in constant battle with it's own self. We become helpless spectators sucked into our internal drama, living a vast majority of our lives inside our heads. If we are to start living 'real' life in the real world, we need to show our prowess once again to pull ourselves out of the quagmire of our inner maze.

It is time for the next stage of evolution.

The Good Destruction

Sometimes
meaningful
destruction
is better than
senseless creation.

Happiness hurts

The sound of your silence
The scar of your glance
The touch of your presence
Takes me deep in a trance

The whispers of your thoughts
Keeps echoing in my mind
I fill the empty walls
Writing your name next to mine

They said love will make it better
Its light will shine my world
But instead it's your presence
That's causing my happiness to hurt.

All the Valid Reasons

There were many valid reasons
why you could not
I was hoping you would find one
So that you could.

The Old Connection

However old, independent, and successful we may have become, it always feels good and reassuring to reconnect with our younger selves, reminisce about who we once were, what motivated us, what felt important to us, and what made us happy. Going down that memory lane once in a while is not only sentimental and enriching but also rejuvenating.

The easiest way to do so is to connect with an old friend, who has the audacity, right, and love, to pull us down to the ground from the height of our stature and reunite us with our roots.

The Flight

We take flights all the time.
But the question is, how often we take them to meet
someone and how often we take them
to leave someone behind.

From Pebbles to Mountain

There is a sense of comfort, assurance, and optimism in the simplicity of aggregating the countless trivia in order to build something significant. It makes a laborious task of creating something meaningful appear less daunting.

It doesn't matter how tiny each pebble is or how many of them there are, as long as we keep piling them up one at a time, a mountain is bound to emerge from their shadows.

To that extent, nothing is ever insignificant. A pebble just needs to find the right mountain to carry upon its tiny shoulders.

Facing the Unfamiliar

I need to say this
To myself and to you
So we both know how my world
May seem different from your view

The line that I had etched
As I lived my life and grew
Melted away to open up
A door I never knew

It paved a different path
I had never travelled before
Making way for the first step
And the rest to walk alone

My thoughts that had left me
In the moments of elation
Returned in the wake of daylight
With a vengeance of damnation

But I guess one deals alone
With cards and their faces shown
For the hands that dealt them to me
Were nobody's but my very own.

To Be or Not To Be

If I try to be perfect, then it's really not me anymore. I never was and never will be perfect, because the mere definition of it keeps evading. Perfection can be as real as a mirage.

All I really want is to be whoever it is that I choose to be, but to be it with passion. For me, that's as close as it can ever get to being perfect.

It's Always There

We may be too naive, lazy, or frightened to see it,

But there's always a reason.

Always.

Having it All

To all those people who keep telling me that I can't have my cake and eat it too, here are my two cents.

First of all, they got the saying all wrong. The original saying goes likes this... 'to eat your cake and have it too'.

Second of all, why the heck would I bake a cake in the first place, if I can't eat it?

Turbulence

Sometimes,
I don't want a calm and composed heart
For that is too predictable.
Sometimes,
All I want is turbulence.
A turbulence so strong
That keeps my desires roaring
Keeps my dreams soaring
Reminds me that I exist
Jolts me as I resist.
A turbulence so vibrant,
That it takes me beyond mundane
Sprinkling gleam on all that is plain
Makes my heart jump to the sky
And its thumping reach a new high
A turbulence so loud,
That its shout deafens my mind,
That I am not just living, but alive
Takes my breath away to blow
The dust on my crests and troughs.

Anatomy of a Thought

Troubled by a thought? Pull it out in the open.

Inside the mind, it remains mysterious and feeds on negativity. If we do not shield its truth with our biases, we can finally understand it's anatomy.

So pull it out of your head. Lay it flat on the floor and completely expose it so that it can be seen from all the sides and all the angles.

That's when it loses its power.

The Old Trunk

Once upon a time
There was a me

Wandering about in stupor
In the basement of my home
Mindlessly occupied in bringing order
To the labyrinth of mundane chores

With hand full of dust
Mind full of thoughts
I played my favourite game of hop scotch
The hop scotch of my mind

And as I bent to pick up my thought
My hand met with an old wrinkled trunk
They knew each other from a distant past
As they reunited, their distance shrunk

There it was, the old wrinkled trunk.

cont.

Holding colourful rags & knotted yarn
Shiny stones & faded bronze
Broken glasses from when I fell
Torn photos of when I rebelled
Letters written of broken love
Tiny hand prints on baby's glove
Stories I read along with a friend
The one who left me along the bend
All of these, and many such crowns
Raised my being from birth until now

But the trunk knew,
Infinite time will come and go
Shadowed past will often show
Bruises and healing are part of the game
We hide the scars and cover the shame
But to truly adorn, the returning hurt
We must first embrace, its lingering dust

And when I opened the lid some more
I saw an old thought smiling back at me
And just like that on that dusty day
I found a piece of my broken me.

Intellect of Brain and Might of Mind

However traumatic, our physical pain becomes a fleeting memory as soon as the body stops feeling it physically. Afterwards, however hard we may try to stretch our imagination, our brain will not allow our body to feel the pain with the same intensity.

Our mind, on the other hand, without much effort, can bring a past emotional pain back to life at the spur of the moment. It can not only make us feel that pain many times over, but each time, with an intensity far worse than before.

That's the difference between our brain and our mind. If left to our biology and to the intelligence of our brain, it will do it's job of protecting our body the way it is designed by nature.

cont.

However, if left to our mind, it will continue to hurt itself in exchange for the satisfaction of being 'right' and for the pleasure of feeling like a victim.

Imagine how traumatic it would be if we allowed our brain to make us relive the unbearable pain of childbirth, or a traumatic accident, over and over again?

If we would never give that permission to our brains, then why give it to our mind and allow the residue of our pain to linger?

The Departure

It is only after I truly learnt
what it came to teach me,
did the pain
finally depart.

Love is Blind-2

They say love is blind...

Then why does the invisible pain of love
Looks clearer, than its healing touch
Why make the unfamiliar and unknown fear
So important and matter so much

Why be blinded by the lustre & brightness
And not feel its warmth
Why watch with caution, every move made
But miss in that, the grace of a swan

Why long for glimpses of things, paper wrapped
And let the unadorned love, fade away untapped
Why the touch of lips is not enough to seize the heart
Why being together is harder than growing apart

Yet they say love is blind.

Inner Work

How one copes during the times of hardship depends on how much work one has done internally.

Hardships often force people to look within for answers. The brighter we have lit our inner world, the easier it will be to search for these answers.

Healing

To feel the hurt is easy.
It is only after we are done feeling the hurt,
does the most difficult task of healing begins.

The Avalanche

Let's snowball our efforts and create an avalanche.

But before we begin, we must first decide what we want to ride on top of the avalanche and what are we prepared to bury underneath it. Because there will be casualties.

Everything comes at a price.

Moving On

I am holding on to thoughts
Of the time we spent together
These memories that I hide
Will remain with me forever

I know I should move on
But I can't make up my mind
'Cause moving on means
Leaving you behind.

The Right Thing

Sometimes we do the right thing not because doing it makes us feel right, but because not doing it makes us feel more wrong.

Sometimes we do the right thing not out of love but out of being compelled to do so.

Sometimes we do the right thing accidentally without having any real intention of doing it.

Whatever the reason may be, doing the right thing counts - every single time.

Where Force Doesn't Work

We can force someone to do something for us.

We cannot force them to feel something for us.

The Reach of Compassion

Someone once denounced me, "How can you talk about the plight of Syria, or a refugee camp, while sitting in your comfortable home?" I was taken aback by this retort.

In my opinion, one doesn't really have to go anywhere to feel the pain and suffering of others. As human beings, we must have enough compassion within ourselves to feel the shiver of a homeless person even from our heated apartment, to feel the aches of an empty stomach even after having a hearty meal, to feel the pain of a mother who buried her child even after we put our child to sleep on a comfortable bed, and to feel the tragic scars of war, sitting right in our comfortable living rooms.

cont.

Because, if we fail to do even that, how can we ever hope to make any kind of difference in our own small, yet significant way.

As a species, we are slowly losing empathy toward others and becoming too engrossed in our own little myopic version of life.

Our humanness is gathering dust underneath our mundane chaos. And maybe all that is required is a strong blow of compassion to remove that dust, right in the comforts of our living rooms.

Mom, I want to go Home
Plea of a refugee child (abridged)

Home...My sweet home... My lost home

Where I played with stones and papers,
Where friends ran with me from dusk to dawn,
My home of mud and broken bricks,
My home of holes and tattered walls

I laughed at everything then,
Even at the grumbling noises that my stomach made,
The vacuum in my stomach never bothered me,
My childhood was enough to make it all evade

Then one day you told me, we had to go across the sea,
To find a place not covered with a shawl of fire,
Where the earth is green and the sky still blue,
Where I can play without dodging smoke and fire

cont.

I towed my little thoughts filled with big doubts,
Will I have friends there who will play with me?
On the strange tarred streets between the tents,
My new home where I am strangely called a refugee

I see Mom, the blue sky that you promised,
And I see all the colours that I never saw before,
I see here that the earth is like a fairyland,
But I still dream of my old life across the shore

Can I ever go back to my country?
Can I ever see my friends again?
Can I ever play with the games of innocence?
Can I ever touch my home again?

My lost home...My favourite home

Where I played with stones and papers,
Where friends ran with me from dusk to dawn,
My home of mud and broken bricks,
My home of holes and tattered walls.

Sigh !

Sometimes, a single sigh released from the deepest depths of the heart can make us experience an emotion in its most purest and unadulterated form. No words are then necessary.

Forgotten Facts, Remembered Memories

I may not remember all the facts, figures, and stories about most of my travel escapades. And that's not really important. What is important, however, is that when those moments were experienced, they smelt like lavender, sounded like a violin, felt like wet waves, tasted like fresh air, and looked like dew drops. What is important is that these moments engraved their poetry on the pages of my memory.

These experiences, small and big, play their part in subtle, yet definite, ways to carve our individualities. It is the cumulation of all these small moments over a period of our lifetime, that creates the uniqueness shining within each one of us.

If I was moved, even for a few moments, my trip was worth it.

Travel...But..

Traveling helps me discover myself like no other means of exploration. The only requirement is that I must never forget to take myself along.

The Travellers of the World

In a foreign land, when I travel alone, I use every opportunity to interact with the locals as well as other fellow travellers. The more I connect with people, the clearer the simplicity of what we are seeking in the travels of our life becomes.

At the end of the day, all we want is to leave our footprints in unknown territories, quench our thirst with unique experiences, find wonder in the mundane, relish in the food and music of the world, and fill our life with cherished memories. Sometimes we do that by travelling to another land, and sometimes we do that by welcoming outsiders into our space.

In that sense, we are all travellers, those entering a new land, and also those whose lands have been entered.

Out of the Ashes

From the time she is born,
She's chained to the stereotypes
Defined by the society
And for her soul to internalize

She learns to accept and imbibe
These expectations, dos and don'ts
She fights against her dreams
To make way for someone's ethos

Then one day she wakes up
And finds herself sinking into the swamp
Fighting to breathe she wonders
How she got there, how could she let this carry on

cont.

And so she decides to fight back
But this time for her own destiny
And so begins a long struggle
To find her true identity

What metamorphosis will she need
To float above the surface
What all will she burn
To come out from her ashes

Is she only, one of the few
Enlightened and educated ones?
Or do we also see these ashes
On the veil of a 'mud-woman'

Feminism

For me, feminism starts with having the maturity and wisdom to find one's own definition of true happiness, irrespective of what is socially acceptable. Feminism is about claiming one's right to all the available choices and to then have the mental freedom and courage to choose the one that aligns with personal happiness.

So on the one hand, it may mean going fearlessly after your career despite the judgemental scorns of the 'ideal motherhood club', and on the other hand, it may mean choosing the path of motherhood despite the contemptuous glances of the 'ideal feminist gang'.

Feminism is to go after our truly cherished dreams without falling prey to any ideologies of feminism, sexism, racism, classism, or any other -isms. It is standing up for oneself against the bullies of society, be it a man or another woman.

#metoo

I don't think there's any woman who has not faced
some kind of unwanted sexual gesture, advancement,
or action in public places or within the secure walls of
our homes. Often the sheer number of such occur-
rences makes a woman ignore many of them as a way
of life. You see, we have programmed our minds to
prioritize what we should let go and what we should
take seriously. Otherwise, we will simply go mad.

What does that say about the times we are living in?
What does it say about us women?
What does it say about the generation we are raising?

Standing Up

I must stand for myself first,

before expecting others to stand next to me.

I need to make my own limbs stronger

before reaching out for the crutches.

Negativity in Stride

One of the most valuable lessons that I taught myself is to not take negative opinions personally.

It doesn't matter how involved I may have been in my work, but the moment I present it to another person, I must cut the emotional umbilical cord. I must remind myself that just like this one piece of work is only a small part of my unlimited expression, rejection is also one of the many possible reactions and out-comes. It is directed toward my work and has nothing to do with the person behind the work.

After all, no one task or event can ever completely define who I am as a whole.

What I Know

What I know, is how you make me feel
When your roaming eyes halt on mine
In a room full of faces, of which I feel
The most mundane is mine.
Yet they stay for a moment longer
And then move on, only to return
To steal another glance

It is this very moment, that stirs me from inside
Makes me go weak, and makes it worthwhile
As if it's okay to stay
Just this one time
Just for a while.

What I know, is how you make me feel
When you whisper my name
It feels like waves touching my feet
Only to return from where they came
Leaving behind a residue of its touch
Nothing had till then mattered so much.

cont.

It is this very moment, that stirs me from inside
Makes me go weak, and makes it worthwhile
As if it's okay to stay
Just this one time
Just for a while.

What I know, is how you make me feel
When you move your hands down my hair
I read your thoughts, they make me shiver
You want more, but then you hold back
Your tremors stop me right on my track
It is this very moment, that stirs me from inside
Makes me go weak, and makes it worthwhile

As if it's okay to stay
Just this one time
Just for a while.

Mistaken Love

Some mistake their insecurities and

emotional dependence for love.

Little do they know that it's exactly what love is not.

Immensity

Whenever I want to free myself of the troubling pettiness of my ego, I surround myself with something of such immensity, that it can show my ego how inconsequential it truly is.

And every single time that greatness is the quiet grandeur of nature.

Broken a Little

We are all broken a little
Torn a little
Damaged a little

From the wants of our vices
From the urges of our greed
From the longings of our dreams
From the cravings of our needs

We are all scarred a little

The same shears of wants
That rip the delicate weaves
We now use them as needles
To sew our torn sheets

cont.

And then,
We rest upon these sheets

We rest upon,
Their shreds and their patches
Our wounds and our scratches
Hoping the weight of our burden
Will caress and balm these gashes

But yet again,
We are all broken a little more
Torn a little more
From the wants of our vices
From the urges of our greed
From the longings of our dreams
From the cravings of our needs
We are all
Damaged a little more.

The Worthy Knowledge

If we don't even know our own self,

then what is it that we really know?

What is the point of knowing anything else?

The Realities of our Lives

If given an honest chance to reveal themselves in their unembellished forms, our realities have the power to bring immense clarity to our little world, even at their own cost, even if it means that we may choose another reality over them. In that regard, they are truly selfless.

After all, they are our realities; they live and die for us.

The rat race to happiness - An essay

The first step towards chasing real happiness causes real misery. The majority of us grew up believing and cherishing the pre-defined parameters of happiness. We believe that the more parameters we can fulfil, the more happiness we can achieve. And thus begins our journey to chase what we are wired to believe. And while we are at it, we don't seem to realize when this personal journey of life becomes a full-fledged rat race.

It's amazing, this rat race.

This is a race where the finishing line is also racing away from us. Irrespective of whether we are the 'hare' or the 'tortoise' in this race, we can never really touch the finish line that keeps teasing and taunting us with 'catch me if you can'.

cont.

It's not a surprise that happiness seems like a mirage.

But then, somewhere along the race, some people notice this paradox. They begin to question the dynamics of this race and the authenticity of the moving goalpost. And something unthinkable happens. Against all the practical wisdom acquired over the years, they do the unthinkable... they Pause.

It's amazing, this Pause.

Somehow this pause is more demanding and challenging than the actual running. But these warriors brave the pause. They begin to realize that if the goal post keeps running faster than them, they will never be able to achieve it. They figure out that their chase for the 'pre-defined' notions of success will not make them happy. They again do the unthinkable.

cont.

They begin to redefine their own meaning of happiness. And thus begins a new journey.

It's amazing, this new journey.

It forces us to carve our own track and field event inside the Olympics of humanity. It makes us look inside for answers, rather than glancing at our neighbours. And as we attempt to accomplish this already arduous task, we, at the same time, have to find the courage to not get lured back to the old race. The old race, by the way, looks like a cakewalk compared to this inner contemplation.

We become like recovering addicts searching for a detox plan hidden under the pool of our vices. Nothing can be more brutally demanding of our undeterred determination than this.

cont.

And then, upon finding some answers that are true to us and our wellness and fulfilment, begins yet another journey.

It's amazing, this new journey.

It is like no other. The goalpost is now steadfast and awaits for us with open arms. This is a journey where traversing becomes like a series of self-choreographed moves, where rhythm becomes more important than the technique.

This is a journey where the steps define the direction. This is a journey where the feet pave the path.

And that's how it should be.

The Step child

Alone in the corner, the step-child waits
Hoping against hope, for the darkness to fade
But the life goes on, with its busy grinding churn
The Step child sits alone, quietly waiting for its turn

Wrapped in your life, trapped in its maze
You give yourself in, to a never-ending chase
You do everything, that the world expects of you
Your family, your friends, and sometimes strangers
too

And then you are left with nothing
Nothing more to give
So far away have you gone
That there's nothing left to feel
For that child who is abandoned
Who's always left behind
The one who always waits
For a tiny grain of your time

cont.

You ignore, you mistreat
You stopped caring long ago
You forgot to remember
The existence of that tiny soul
So busy, so tired, you have no moments
Not even a few
For that lonesome little soul
The step-child that is you.

These were some of my thoughts
that I fished from the ocean.
Some are still floating
on the surface of the waves,
some are still dreaming
deep under it's belly.
Slowly, I will bring them out too,
with some new words
on some new pages

Until then, I thank you for spending time
with my thoughts. And with me.

Thank You

With all my gratitude, I thank you for reading the pages that came before this. You may have disagreed with some of my thoughts resolutely, and with some, perhaps found an equally strong sense of cerebral déjà vu. Some lines may have created ripples in your heart, while some verses may have given your thoughts a silent company.

If any of that happened, my thoughts indeed spoke to yours, and they thank you for being heard.

If you enjoyed reading my book, it would mean a lot to me if you could find time to leave your honest review on the website from where you purchased the book.

I wish you a joyful and fulfilled life.

Yours truly,
Asmita

Instagram: @asmita.rajiv
Website: http://www.asmitarajiv.com
Email: asmita@asmitarajiv.com

I consider myself lucky

Every time an idea begins to take shape in my mind,
I get goosebumps.
Every time I see a blank canvas,
I feel tremors of excitement.
Every time I complete a painting or a poem,
I feel an incredible sense of satisfaction.
And every time I look at my finished work,
Another idea begins to take shape.

What more can I ask for.

A bit about myself

Unlike my formal qualifications in Physics and an MBA, which are backed by formal degrees, my existence as an artist and a poet is purely backed by my passion. A passion so strong, that made me quit my corporate career, stopped me from playing hide and seek with my calling, and taught me the true meaning of the word gratitude. It is with this gratitude, that I paint each stroke and write each line.

When I am not painting or writing, I could be found having a medley of meaningful, deep and utterly non-sensical conversations with my dear ones, cherishing my "me-time", travelling, learning yoga and engaging in my newly found passion for driving on the German Autobahns.

Made in the USA
Middletown, DE
30 April 2023

29767252R00116